AF087622

TRAUMA IS REALLY STRANGE.

This is a classic description of dissociation from David Livingstone, writing in 1857 (Kandel et al 2000). Leading trauma specialist Bessel van der Kolk (2014) states 'Dissociation is the essence of trauma.' After a traumatic event people often drift in and out of dissociation.

James Rhodes (2015), pianist and sexual abuse survivor, states dissociation is 'The most serious and long-lasting of all the symptoms of abuse...ever since then, like a Pavlov puppy, the minute a feeling or situation even threatens to become overwhelming, I am no longer there.'

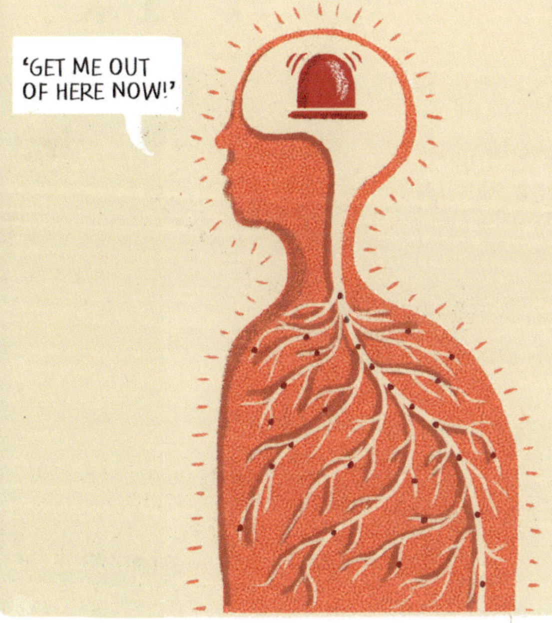

A common response is contracting to make ourselves small, ultimately into an immobile, fetal position. We are left bracing ourselves against life, disconnected from our internal and external worlds. 'Trauma occurs when an event creates an unresolved impact on an organism' (Levine 1997).

Running away from a lion is life or death. All non-essential activity is switched off, there is no need for digestion, libido and reproduction, immune system, or growth and repair (Sapolsky 2004). Health can dramatically improve when the 'defense cascade' is reset (Kozlowska et al 2015).

LET'S LOOK AT SOME STATEMENTS FROM CLINICAL PRACTICE THAT DEMONSTRATE THE STRANGENESS OF TRAUMA.

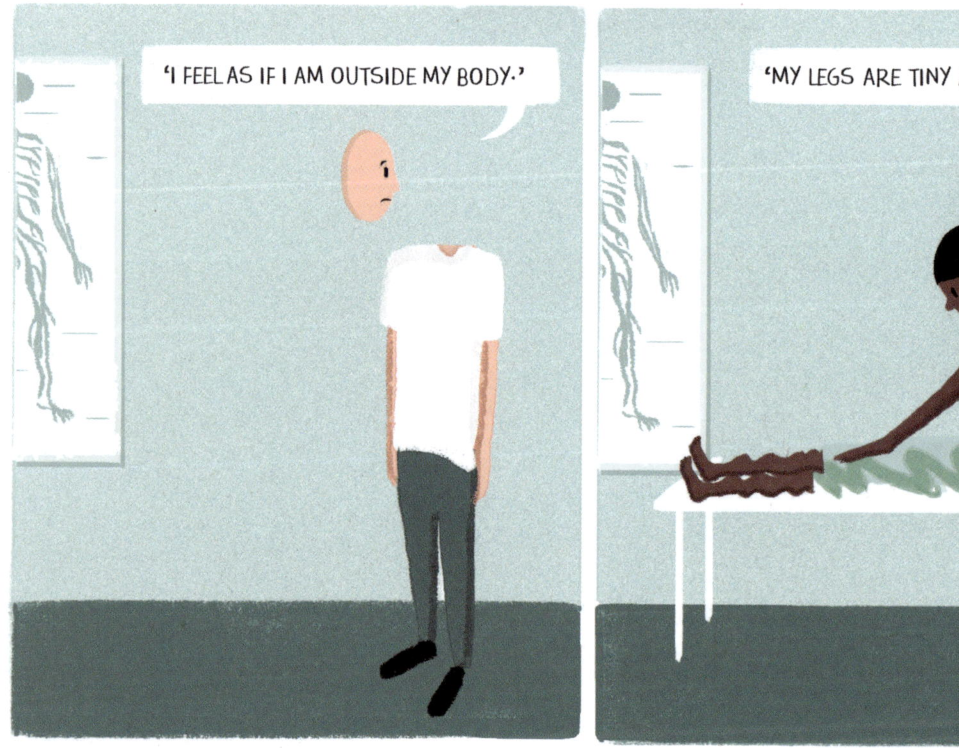

'I FEEL AS IF I AM OUTSIDE MY BODY.'

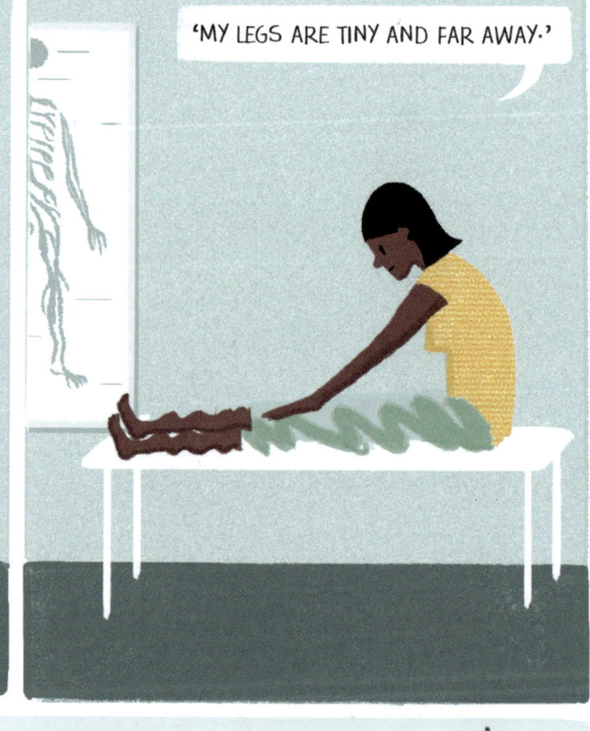

'MY LEGS ARE TINY AND FAR AWAY.'

ALSO, DISSOCIATION...
CAN MAKE US...
A BIT CLUTZY!

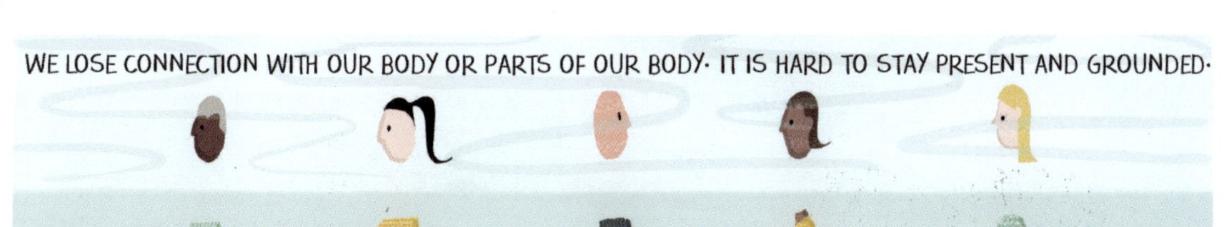

WE LOSE CONNECTION WITH OUR BODY OR PARTS OF OUR BODY. IT IS HARD TO STAY PRESENT AND GROUNDED.

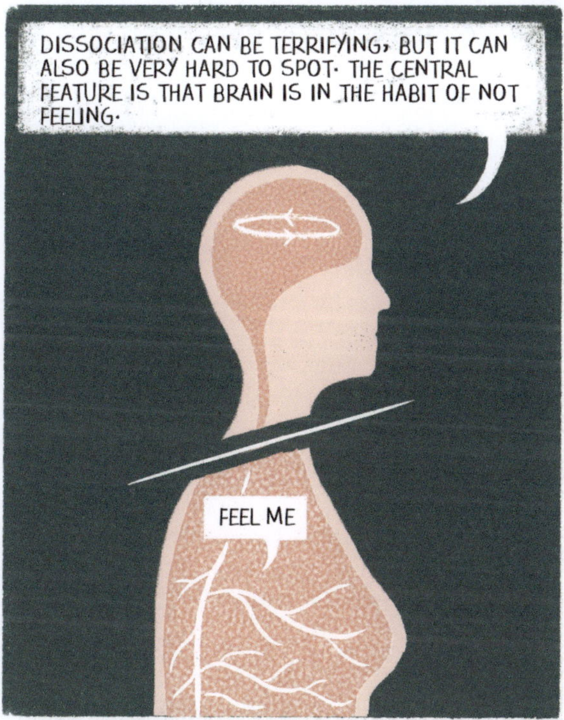

DISSOCIATION CAN BE TERRIFYING, BUT IT CAN ALSO BE VERY HARD TO SPOT. THE CENTRAL FEATURE IS THAT BRAIN IS IN THE HABIT OF NOT FEELING.
FEEL ME

DISSOCIATION IS DIFFICULT TO IDENTIFY AS 'WE DON'T KNOW WHAT WE DON'T KNOW.' OLD PARTS OF THE BRAIN ARE TRYING TO STOP US SENSING, DISTANCING US FROM THE BODY AND LIMITING OUR PERCEPTION.

PEOPLE CAN RELY ON THINKING AND FUNCTION PRETTY WELL, BUT OFTEN REPORT THEY FEEL CUT OFF, LIKE AN OBSERVER.

'I CAN'T GET ENOUGH AIR IN.'

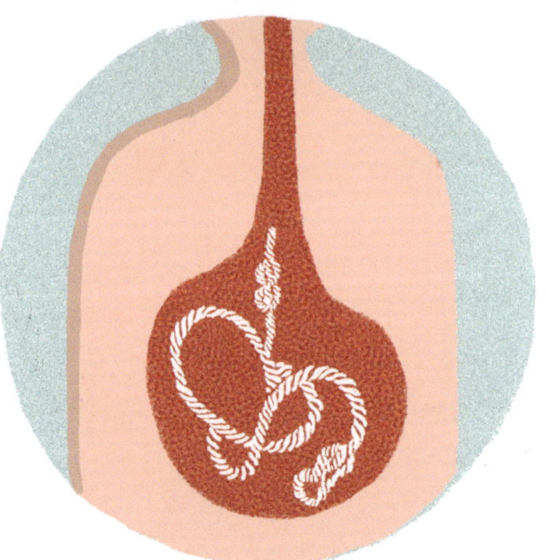

'THERE IS A KNOT OF ANXIETY IN MY BELLY.'

'THOUGHTS KEEP INVADING ME, IT'S AN OBSESSION I CANNOT LET GO OF.'

'I CAN'T KEEP STILL, MY MIND IS RACING.'

Classic post-traumatic stress disorder (PTSD) symptoms include involuntarily re-experiencing aspects of the traumatic event in a very vivid and distressing way, avoidance behaviour, hyperarousal and emotional numbing (NICE 2005).

Being stuck in fast forward can be very productive. There are many successful executives whose internal state drives them forward. But the imperative from the body is ultimately very draining and frequently associated with massive anxiety.

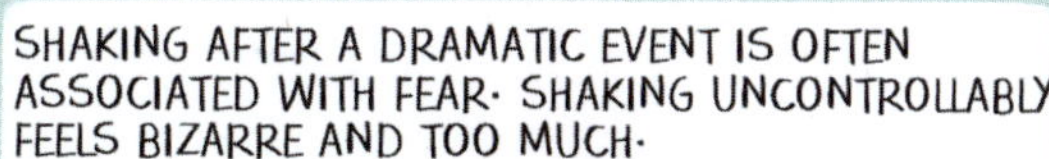

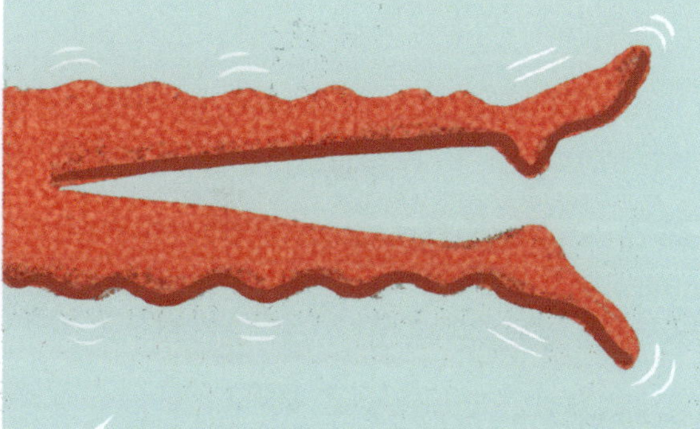

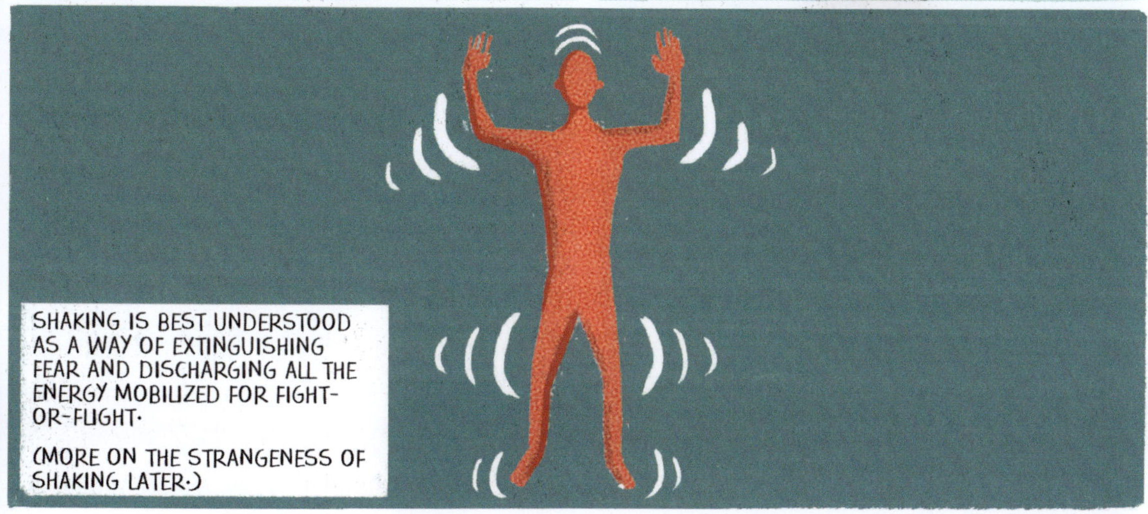

The 'I'm shaking, is this normal?' quote is from a young girl after watching her first deer be killed. Her dad does an amazing job of reassuring her and helping her discharge, check YouTube: 'Savannah's first deer hunt'.

The amount of people who experience restless leg syndrome (RLS) is surprisingly high: 'RLS affects 5%–10% of adults in the general population, and is associated with various chronic conditions' (Li et al 2013).

'As I learned more about how people manage to withstand extremely aversive events, it became all the more apparent to me that humans are wired to survive. Not every-body manages well, but most of us do' (Bonanno 2010).

These three statements are drawn from the work of Dr David Berceli, creator of Trauma Releasing Exercises (TRE). The body is central to healing, as often 'there are no words to describe the depth of human experience the trauma survivor has been plunged into' (Berceli 2008a).

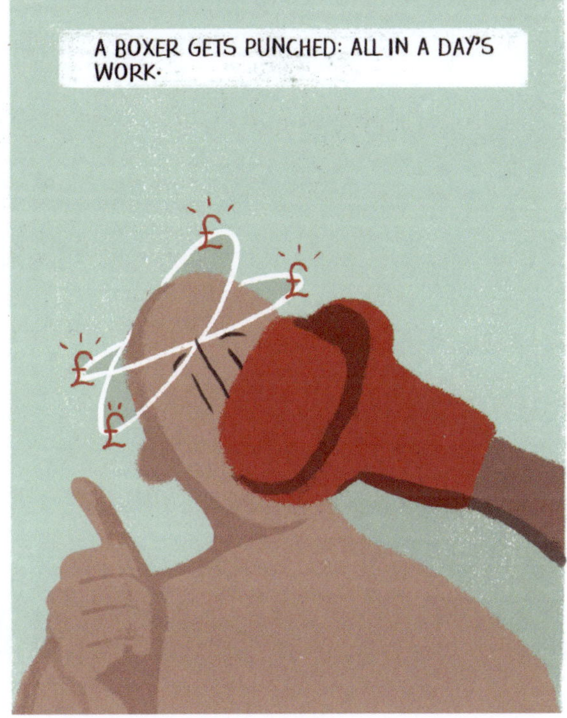

The definition of trauma is drawn from the work of trauma expert Peter Levine (1997). Defining trauma is complex and political. van der Kolk (2014) describes a battle to get the diagnosis PTSD accepted by American psychiatrists in the 1980s.

van der Kolk (2014) is scathing on the failure to include 'Complex PTSD' and 'Developmental Trauma Disorder' in diagnostic manuals. PTSD descriptions focus on sudden threatening events and injury, with consequences of intrusive thoughts, avoidance behaviour and increased arousal.

'For every soldier who serves in a war zone abroad, there are ten children endangered in their own homes' and 'The consequences of caregiver abuse and neglect is vastly more common and more complex than the impact of hurricanes or motor vehicle accidents' (van der Kolk 2014).

In the space of a short comic book it is hard to do justice to the many terrible things that can overwhelm human beings. Focusing on our resilience and ability to endure is in no way meant to underplay the suffering and complexity of surviving intense fear, helplessness or horror.

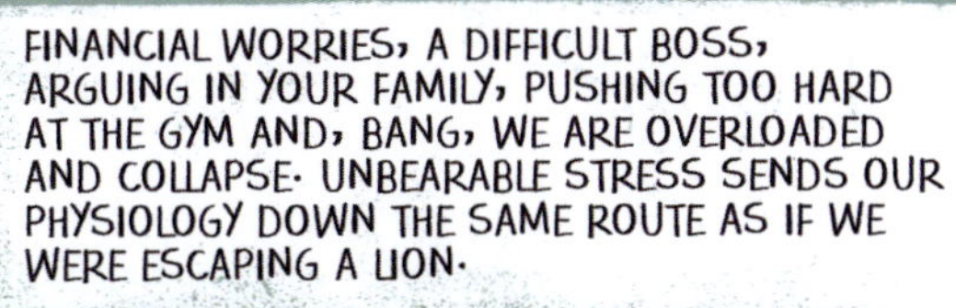

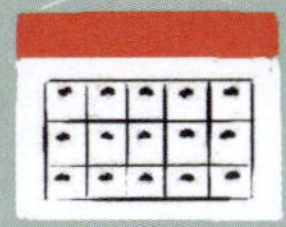

Another cause of overwhelm: people such as family members, carers, social workers, therapists, or first responders to emergencies can experience 'vicarious trauma' as they observe, empathize with and mirror the pain of others (Figley 2005).

'The stress-response can become more damaging that the stressor itself.' Stress-related diseases and 'psychological uproar' emerge by continually turning on 'a physiological system that has evolved for responding to acute physical emergencies' (Sapolsky 2004).

IT IS HOPEFULLY CLEAR BY NOW THAT TRAUMA CAN BE DUE TO MUCH MORE THAN SINGLE DRAMATIC EVENTS.

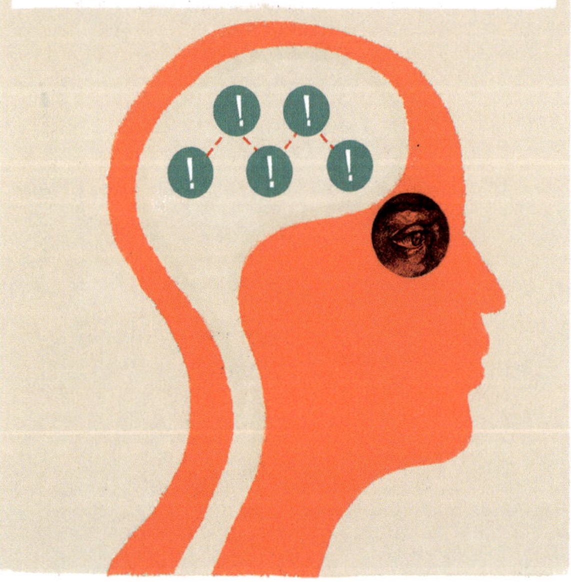

SOME OF OUR MOST IMPORTANT EXPERIENCES OCCURRED BEFORE WE WERE ABLE TO MAKE CLEAR MEMORIES.

BEING BORN MAY BE ONE OF THE TOUGHEST THINGS YOU EVER DID.

BIRTH IS AN EARLY DEFINING STORY THAT LEAVES AN IMPRINT THAT IS OUTSIDE OF CONSCIOUS AWARENESS.

BEING BORN CAN BE A JOYFUL COMING INTO POWER.

BUT FREQUENTLY IT CAN BE A STRUGGLE, WHERE IMPRINTS OF FIGHTING, BEING STUCK, DISPPEARING OR NOT GETTING THE RIGHT HELP ARE ENCODED IN OUR BODY INTELLIGENCE.

BIRTH STORIES GO DEEP. THEY CAN BE HEALED BY LOVE AND CONTACT AND STRONG BONDING WITH PARENTS, BUT ATTACHMENT PROCESSES CAN BE LESS THAN IDEAL.

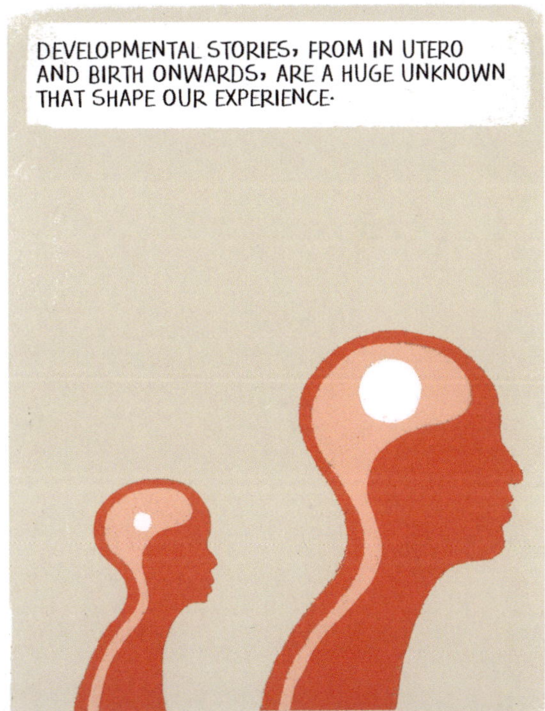
DEVELOPMENTAL STORIES, FROM IN UTERO AND BIRTH ONWARDS, ARE A HUGE UNKNOWN THAT SHAPE OUR EXPERIENCE.

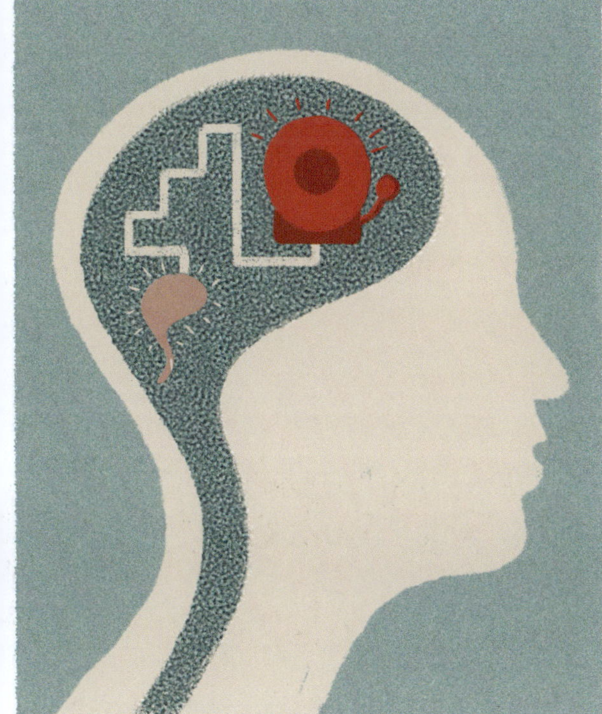
HOW WE BLINDLY FIRST RESPONDED TO EARLY EVENTS BECOMES THE DEFAULT FOR HOW WE RESPOND IN THE FUTURE.

BRAINS ARE SIMPLE LIKE THAT.

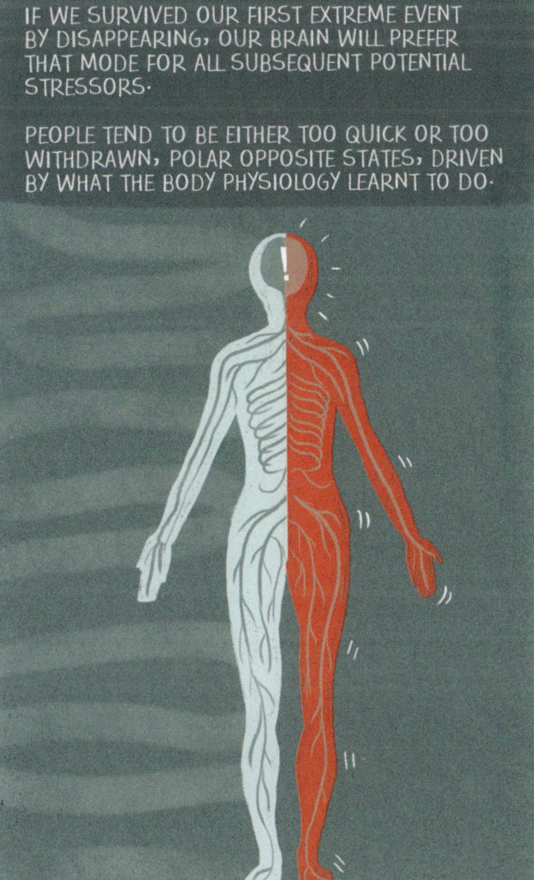
IF WE SURVIVED OUR FIRST EXTREME EVENT BY DISAPPEARING, OUR BRAIN WILL PREFER THAT MODE FOR ALL SUBSEQUENT POTENTIAL STRESSORS.

PEOPLE TEND TO BE EITHER TOO QUICK OR TOO WITHDRAWN, POLAR OPPOSITE STATES, DRIVEN BY WHAT THE BODY PHYSIOLOGY LEARNT TO DO.

'WE CAN OVERCOME TRAUMA.' THE CENTRAL MESSAGE FROM TRAUMA RESEARCH IS THAT HUMANS ARE VERY RESILIENT.
'WE ARE GENETICALLY ENCODED TO KNOW THAT WE WILL EXPERIENCE TRAUMA IN LIFE, THAT WE ARE ABLE TO ENDURE TRAUMA IN LIFE AND THAT WE CAN IN FACT RECOVER FROM TRAUMA.
IF THAT WAS NOT POSSIBLE WE WOULD HAVE DIED AS A SPECIES. TRAUMA HAS ACTUALLY BEEN PART OF OUR EVOLUTIONARY PROCESS.' DR DAVID BERCELI.

STUDYING COMMUNTIES OR GROUPS AFFECTED BY A SINGLE DISASTER, IT HAS BECOME CLEAR THAT 9 OUT OF 10 PEOPLE WILL NATURALLY LEARN AND GROW FROM THE EXPERIENCE.
THE INITAL FOCUS ON SIMPLY DEFINING AND RECOGNIZING PTSD HAS SHIFTED TO MODELS OF 'POST-TRAUMATIC GROWTH', WHERE MOST OF US ARE TEMPERED IN THE FIRE OF EXPERIENCE.
WE CAN, AND FREQUENTLY DO, EMERGE STRONGER AND WISER AFTER BEING OVERWHELMED.

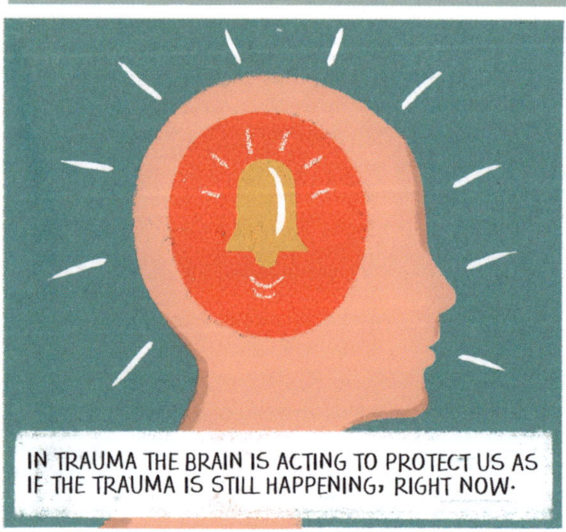

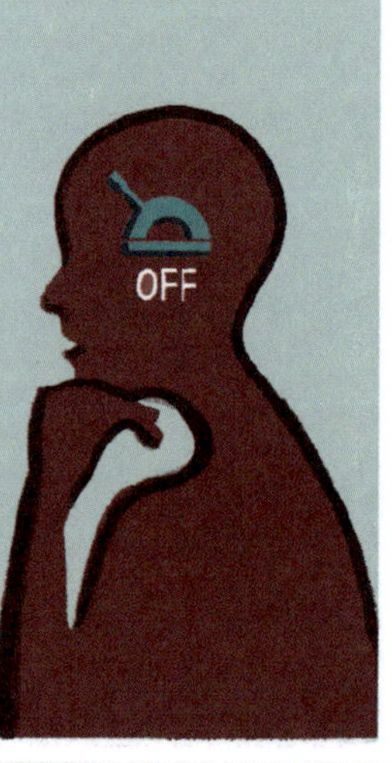

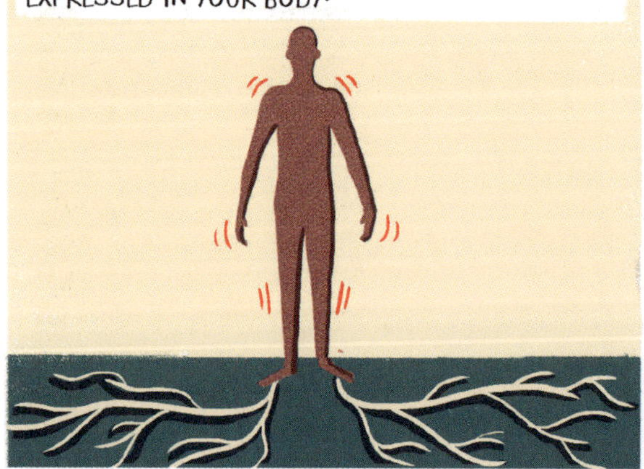

In his book on post-traumatic growth, Professor Stephen Joseph (2013) states that 'On average, only 8–12 per cent of people exposed to traumatic events – and around a fifth to a quarter of those involved in profoundly traumatic experiences – ever reach the diagnostic threshold for PTSD.'

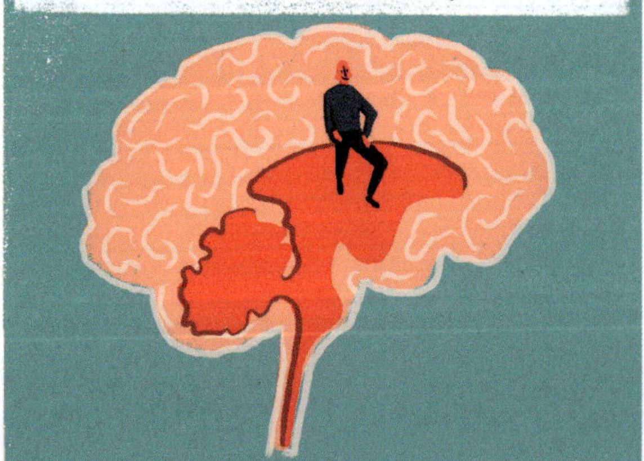

'I believe that the people who are the most resilient, and find the greatest peace in their lives, have learned to tolerate extreme sensations while gaining the capacity for reflective self-awareness' (Levine 2010). Quote on previous page is from the founder of TRE, Berceli 2008b.

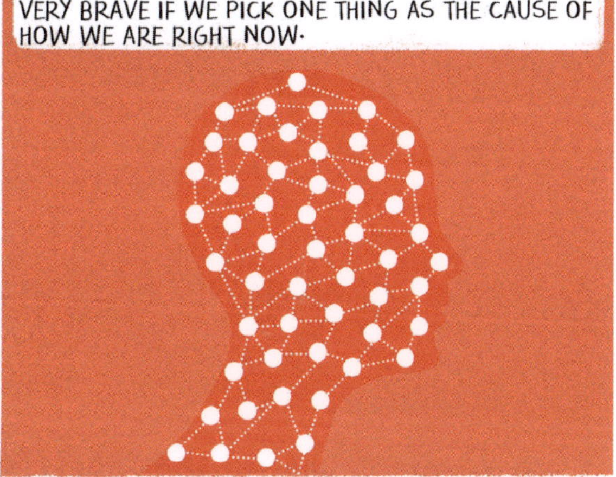

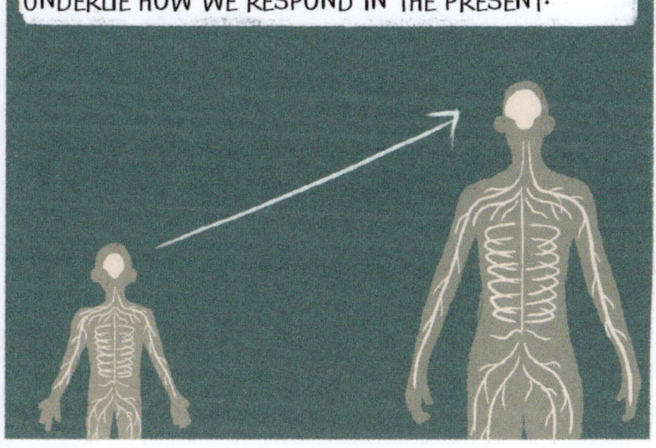

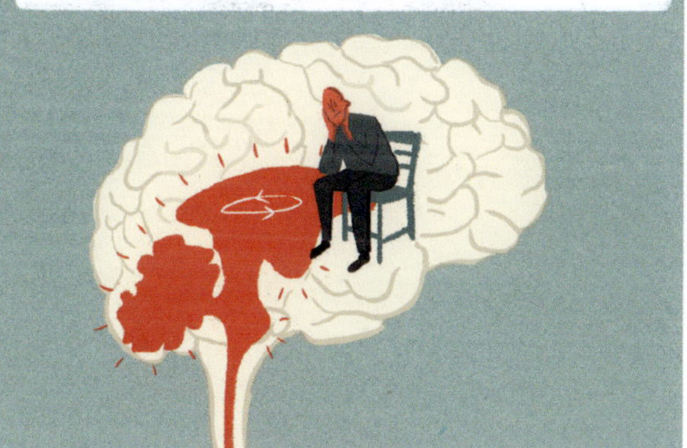

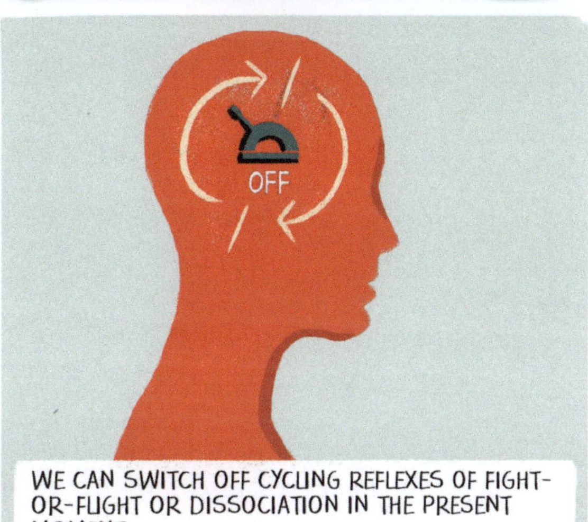

'In the initial stages of restorative work, bottom-up processing needs to be standard operating procedure' (Levine 2010). Talking can be an important part of healing, but you as a whole organism do not truly change until your body comes to life and comes out of danger mode.

Many therapists are puzzled by clients whose early, unknown developmental history taught them to dissociate. This is coupled with a host of confusing physical and emotional symptoms leaking into their lives that can, however, be traced back to over-activated threat defense strategies.

LET'S LOOK MORE AT HOW THE BRAIN WORKS. SO FAR WE HAVE USED THE TERM 'OLD PARTS OF THE BRAIN' TO DESCRIBE THE REGIONS THAT TRIGGER SURVIVAL RESPONSES.

A SIMPLE BUT USEFUL MODEL IS THE 'TRIUNE (THREE-PART) BRAIN'.

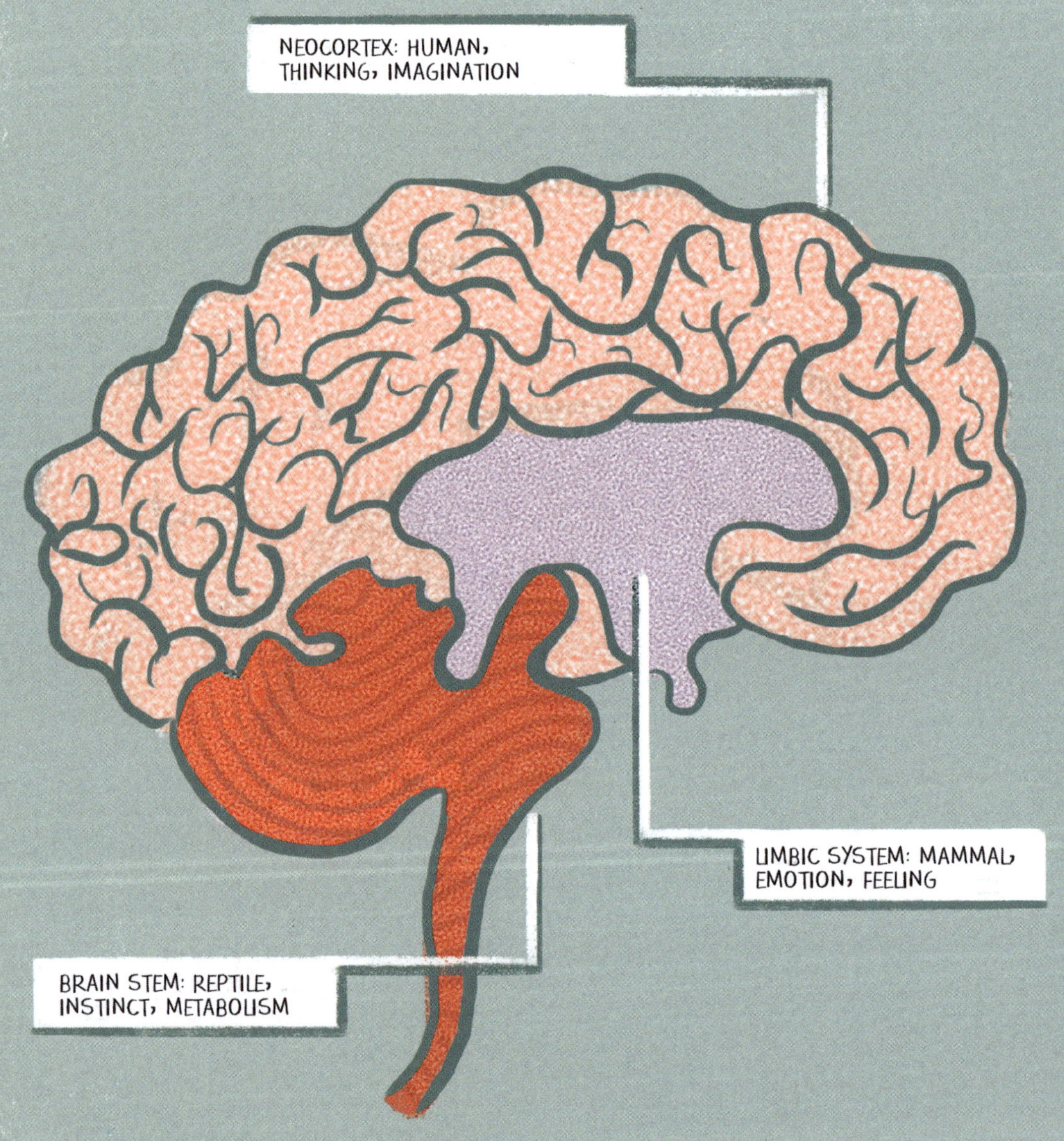

We can also talk of a 'critter brain' (Jacobs 2012), equivalent to the brain stem and limbic system. Other models are 'rational brain versus emotional brain' (van der Kolk 2014), 'thinking fast and slow' (Kahneman 2011) or simply conscious versus unconscious.

The triune brain model was developed by neuroscientist Paul Maclean in the 1960s. 'This three-layered conceptualization helps us grasp the overall function of higher brain areas better than any other scheme yet devised' (Panksepp 1998).

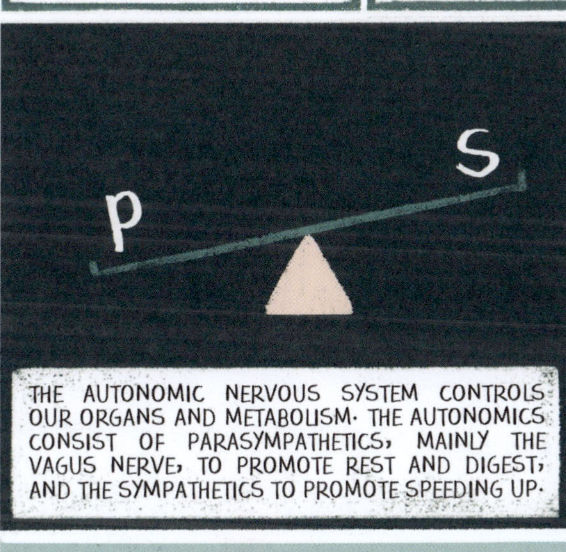

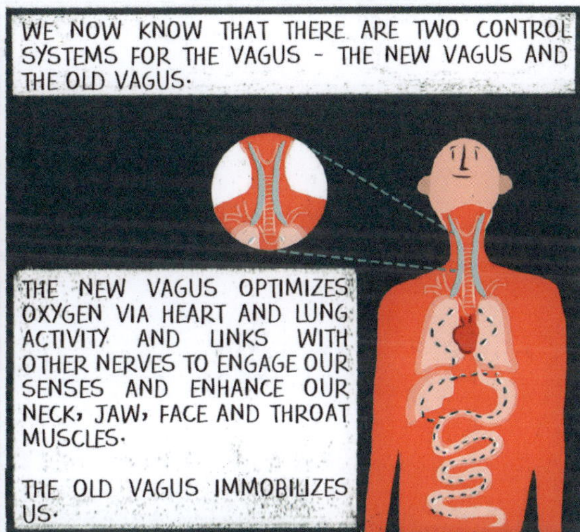

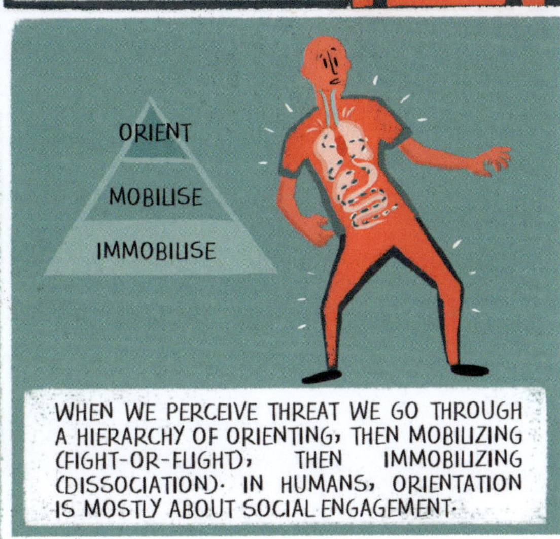

Professor Stephen Porges (2011) developed 'polyvagal theory'. It explains how social interactions are essential negotiations in helping brains find safety. Emotion researcher Dacher Keltner (2009) coined the term 'vagal superstars'.

Orientation, seeking social engagement, is a powerful first response humans have to threat. We learn safety from caregivers. Think of a crying baby: the soft voice, slow, gentle touch and eye contact from their mother, and simply being in that relationship, all switch off the alarm systems.

When we are safe and present, our creativity and capacity for love can flourish. The control of our heart and breathing is optimized by the new vagus and we can express our emotions in a wide variety of ways. The new vagus inhibits fear responses (Porges 2011).

An increasing amount of threat begins to change the activity of our body and our emotional tone. The new vagus begins to fire less – we remove the 'vagal brake' (Thayer and Lane 2000) – and patterns of turning our head and changing our heart rate emerge, followed by fight-or-flight.

IF THE MOUSE GETS CAUGHT, IT IS INESCAPABLE THREAT. WITH NO ESCAPE OPTIONS, IMMOBILIZING HAS PROVED TO BE A USEFUL EVOLUTIONARY STRATEGY. PLAYING DEAD IS AN OLD VAGUS, REPTILIAN REFLEX.

PREDATORS NEED THE THRILL OF THE STRUGGLE TO STAY ENGAGED. OFTEN CATS LOSE INTEREST AND PAUSE; THIS CAN BE AN OPPORTUNITY FOR THE MOUSE TO MOBILIZE AGAIN.

IF THERE IS NO ESCAPE, THE NATURAL OPIOIDS SECRETED BY THE NERVOUS SYSTEM LIMIT THE PAIN OF DEATH AND INDUCE A DREAMY QUALITY (REMEMBER DAVID LIVINGTONE'S STUPOR).

IN HUMANS, EXCESSIVE OPIOIDS CAN LEAD TO A PLEASANT, SPACEY QUALITY OR A TERRIFYING LOSS OF CONTACT WITH REALITY. THIS CAN BE AN INHERENTLY CONFUSING, FREQUENTLY DEPRESSING, LOST PLACE.

DISSOCIATION IS ONE OF THE BIGGEST PRECURSORS TO GETTING LOST IN TRAUMA RESPONSES. THE INABILITY TO FEEL THE BODY AND LACK OF CONNECTION TO OUR INTERNAL EXPERIENCE OFTEN LEADS TO PAIN AND DEPRESSION.

IN TRAUMA, THE WHOLE AUTONOMIC NERVOUS SYSTEM IS STUCK IN COMPETING DEFENSE STRATEGIES. THERE CAN BE WILD SWINGS IN MOOD AND ENERGY. SHOULD I GO QUICK OR SHOULD I DISAPPEAR?

'So I leave my body, floating out of it and up to the ceiling, where I watch myself until it becomes too much even from there, and then I fly out of the room, straight to the closed doors and off to safety. It was an inexplicably brilliant feeling' (Rhodes 2015).

An aside: many spiritual seekers mistake endorphin rushes for transcendental experiences – actually they are dissociating. 'Deep embodiment' is a pre-requisite for authentic experiences of 'flow states' and heightened consciousness (Kotler 2013). See also bit.ly/mouse-escape-video.

The metaphor of the amygdala as a smoke detector is from van der Kolk (2014). The amygdala 'is part of a threat detection system' (LeDoux 2015). Neuroception is the name for threat detection without awareness.

Neuroception 'describes how neural circuits distinguish whether situations or people are safe, dangerous, or life threatening. It explains why a baby coos at a care-giver but cries at a stranger' (Porges 2004).

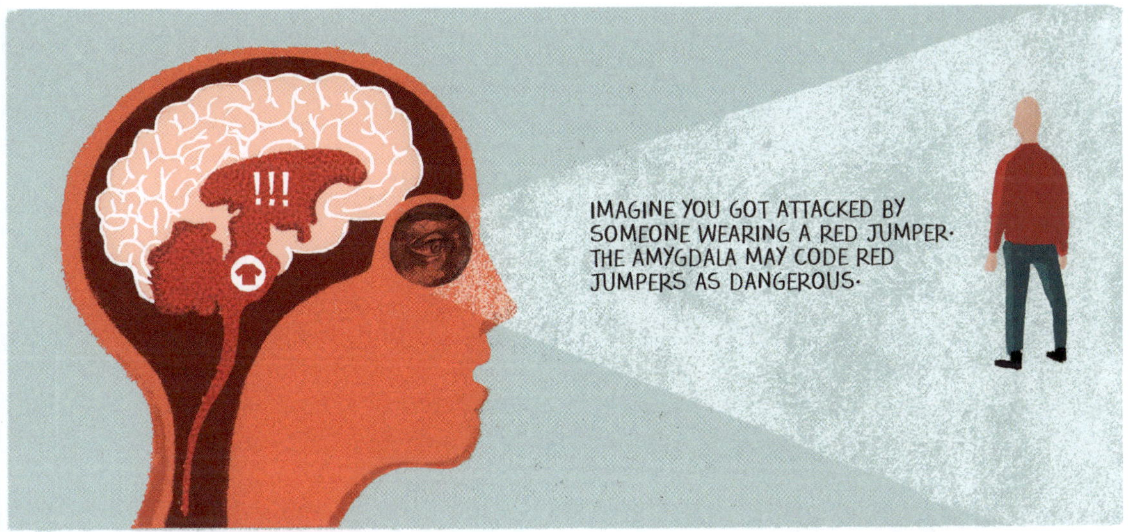

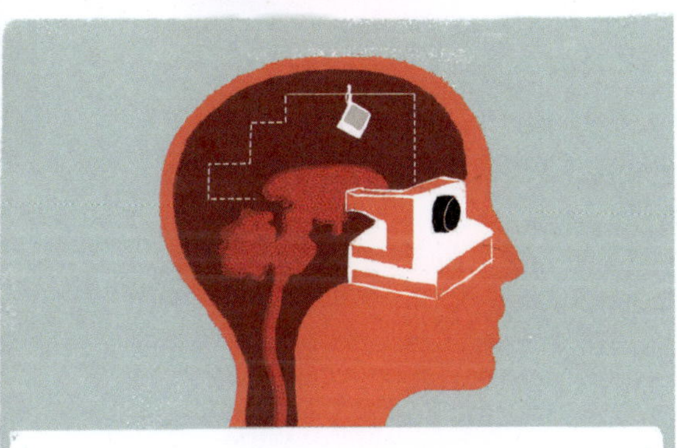

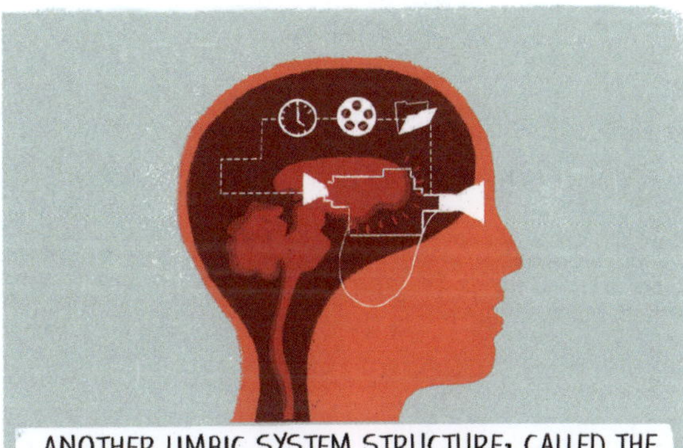

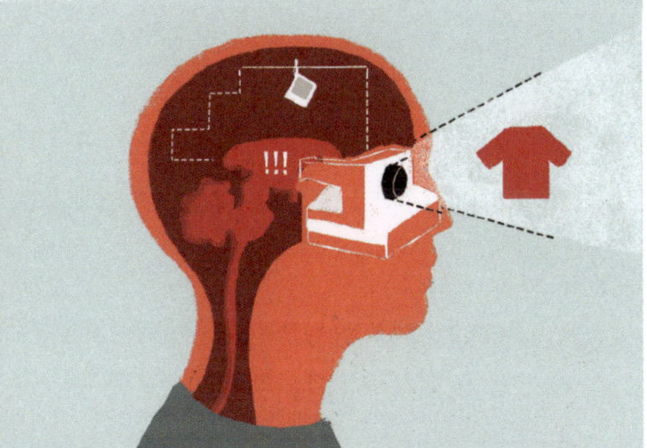

THE HIPPOCAMPUS SHOULD COME ALONG AND PUT A BRAKE ON, SAYING 'THAT WAS 10 YEARS AGO!' TRAUMA IS A FAILURE OF THE HIGH MEGAPIXEL HIPPOCAMPUS TO UPDATE THE BLURRY POLAROID AMYGDALA TO THE PRESENT.

WE CAN HAVE MANY UNCONSCIOUS TRIGGERS THAT SEND OUR PHYSIOLOGY INTO OVERDRIVE. OH DEAR.

The amygdala helps create 'implicit' memories; for example, conditional learning, gut feelings and riding a bike. The hippocampus should provide a timeline and regulate implicit memories, but 'stress hormones (cortisol) suppress the activity of the hippocampus' (Rothschild 2000).

'Prolonged exposure to stress levels of glucocorticoids (cortisol) atrophy hippocampal neuronal processes and, ultimately, cause neuron loss. ... sustained exposure to elevated glucocorticoid concentrations disrupts memory' (Saplosky et al 2000).

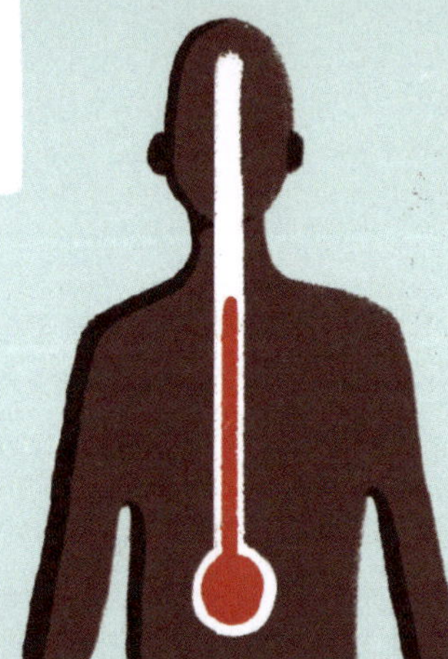

Titration is a concept used by Levine (1997). Titration is a term from chemistry for the slow addition of a known chemical to an unknown solution and the observation of the change. A perfect model, then, for working with the charge of trauma: go slow, take small steps and observe.

'You can be fully in charge of your life only if you acknowledge the reality of your body, in all its visceral dimensions'; 'In order to overcome trauma, you need help to get back in touch with your body, with your Self' (van der Kolk 2014).

The coke bottle model is from Babette Rothschild (2000). 'Containment, it must be understood, is not suppression; it is rather building a larger, more resilient vessel to hold these difficult affects' (Levine 2010).

'Focus not only on regulating the intense memories activated by trauma but also on restoring a sense of agency, engagement, and commitment through ownership of body and mind' (van der Kolk 2014).

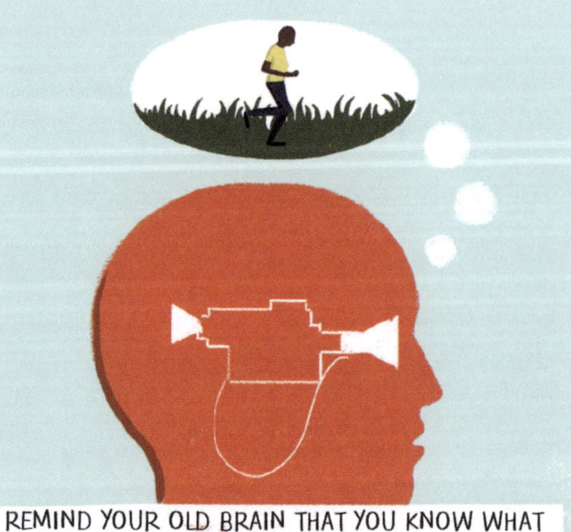

Professional help and support groups can be essential to provide stability in difficult times. Resources and help can come in many forms. Perserverance and hope in seeking the right way for you to be supported is difficult, but the payoff can be enormous.

'I don't think patients, survivors, victimized people can recover in isolation. They need other people and they need to take action in affiliation with others.' The antidote to 'the abuse of power and authority' is the 'solidarity of resistance' (Herman 2000).

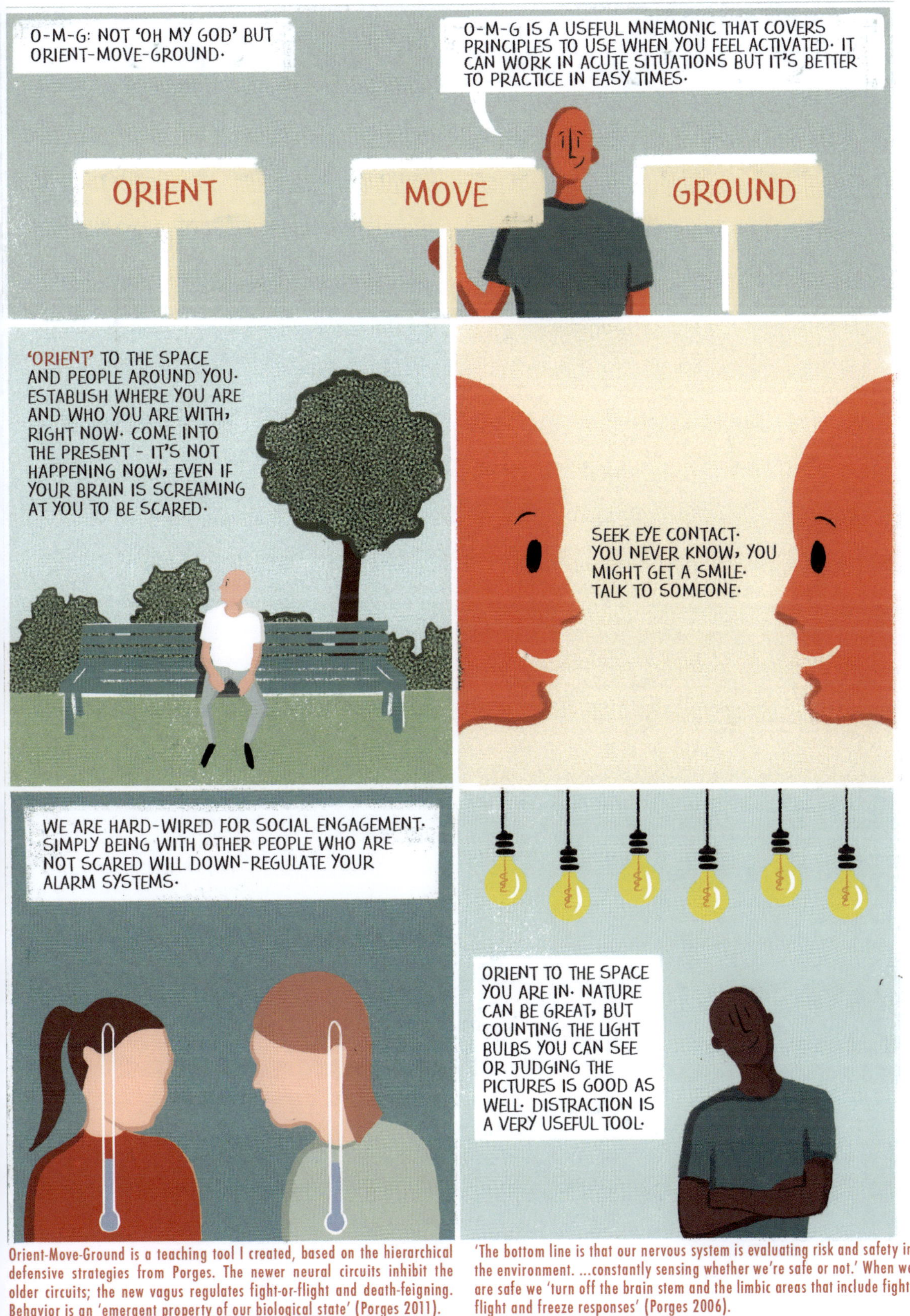

Orient-Move-Ground is a teaching tool I created, based on the hierarchical defensive strategies from Porges. The newer neural circuits inhibit the older circuits; the new vagus regulates fight-or-flight and death-feigning. Behavior is an 'emergent property of our biological state' (Porges 2011).

'The bottom line is that our nervous system is evaluating risk and safety in the environment. ...constantly sensing whether we're safe or not.' When we are safe we 'turn off the brain stem and the limbic areas that include fight, flight and freeze responses' (Porges 2006).

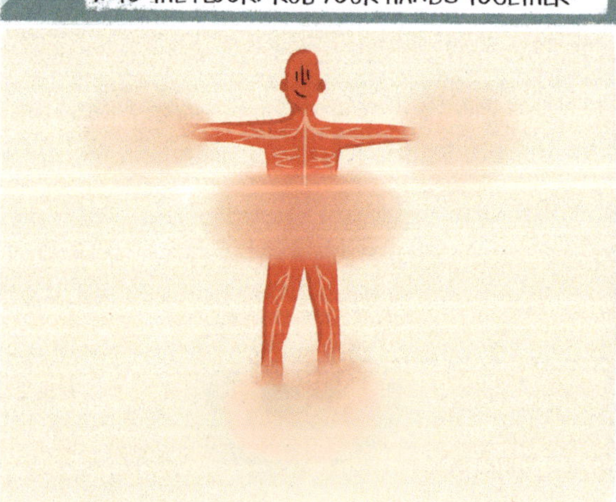

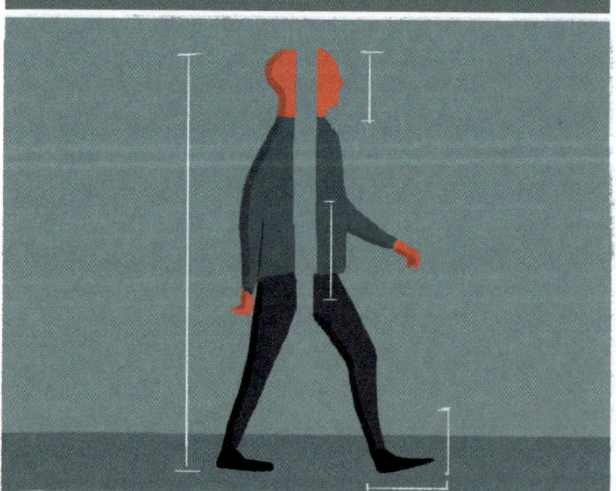

Levine (2010) is very keen on completing the 'instinctual imperative that was thwarted… We have to help clients discover just where in her body she readied for action, and which action had been blocked in its execution.' We are left braced or collapsed in trauma.

'"Grounded" means that you can feel your butt in your chair, see the light coming through the window, feel the tension in your calves, and hear the wind stirring in the tree outside' (van der Kolk 2014). Check the wonderful Amy Cuddy (2012) TED talk on making yourself big.

SHAKING IS SOMETHING THAT HAS TRADITIONALLY BEEN SEEN AS A SYMPTOM AND AS A PATHOLOGICAL RESULT OF TRAUMA.

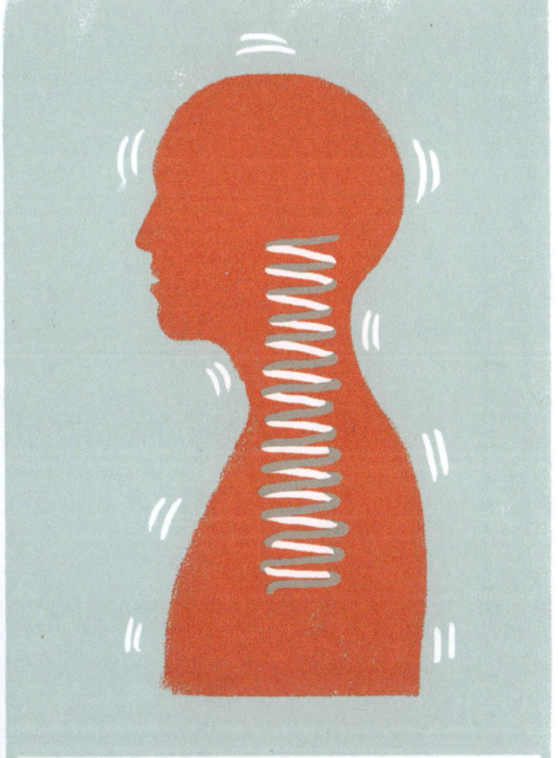

IT TURNS OUT THAT IS A MISCONCEPTION. WE DO NOT SHAKE BECAUSE WE ARE TRAUMATIZED, WE SHAKE BECAUSE IT IS A NATURAL MECHANISM IN THE BODY TO OPTIMIZE TENSION.

TRY TO STAND PERFECTLY STILL. IT IS NOT POSSIBLE. OUR MUSCLES ARE CONSTANTLY CHANGING THEIR TONE AS WE DANCE WITH GRAVITY. LOW LEVEL OSCILLATIONS IN POSTURAL MUSCLES (A FANCY WAY OF SAYING SHAKING) IS NORMAL.

IF WE ARE STRESSED WE DO NOT CONTROL THESE TREMORS VERY ACCURATELY. SOMETIMES THEY GO INTO A POSITIVE FEEDBACK LOOP AND WE VISIBLY SHAKE A LOT.

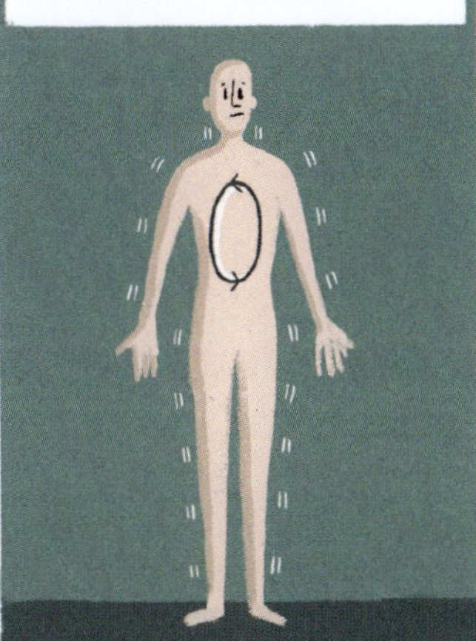

HOWEVER, IF WE CAN BE CURIOUS ABOUT TREMORS AND INTERACT WITH THEM, THE INFORMATION FLOW BETWEEN MUSCLES AND NERVOUS SYSTEM HELPS THE BRAIN RESET THE TONE IN MUSCLES. SHAKING CAN DISCHARGE EXCESS TENSION AND WAKE UP FROZEN BITS OF THE BODY.

TRE is a wonderful self-regulation tool devised by Dr David Berceli. He discovered a simple way to self induce therapeutic tremors. 'Exercises that produce tremors bypass the thinking brain, giving us direct access to the unconscious reptilian brain' (Berceli 2008a).

In TRE a series of seven exercises tire out some of the big muscles in the hips. With encouragement, practice and curiosity it is possible to turn on and turn off shaking in the pelvis and, eventually, all over the body. The tremors in TRE help to reboot the nervous system.

THE VERY NATURE OF TRAUMA IS THAT IT IS OVERWHELMING. IT IS MORE THAN THE ORGANISM CAN COPE WITH.

TRAUMA SHATTERS OUR WORLD VIEW. RULES OF FAIRNESS AND JUSTICE NO LONGER SEEM TO APPLY. TRAUMA OFTEN LEADS TO A SPIRITUAL CRISIS AND A PROFOUND RE-EVALUATION OF MEANING.

TRAUMA TAKES US TO VERY PRIMITIVE PLACES OF FIGHT-OR-FLIGHT OR DISSOCIATION. IT IS VERY HARD TO LIVE FULLY WITH OUR BRAIN SCREAMING 'DANGER!' AND GENERATING LIFE OR DEATH SCENARIOS AT THE SLIGHTEST STIMULUS.

IT IS REALLY IMPORTANT TO FIND A COMMUNITY AND GET SUPPORT TO REDISCOVER WHAT SAFETY FEELS LIKE. TAKE SOME CHANCES AND OPEN UP TO YOUR FRIENDS AND LOVED ONES.

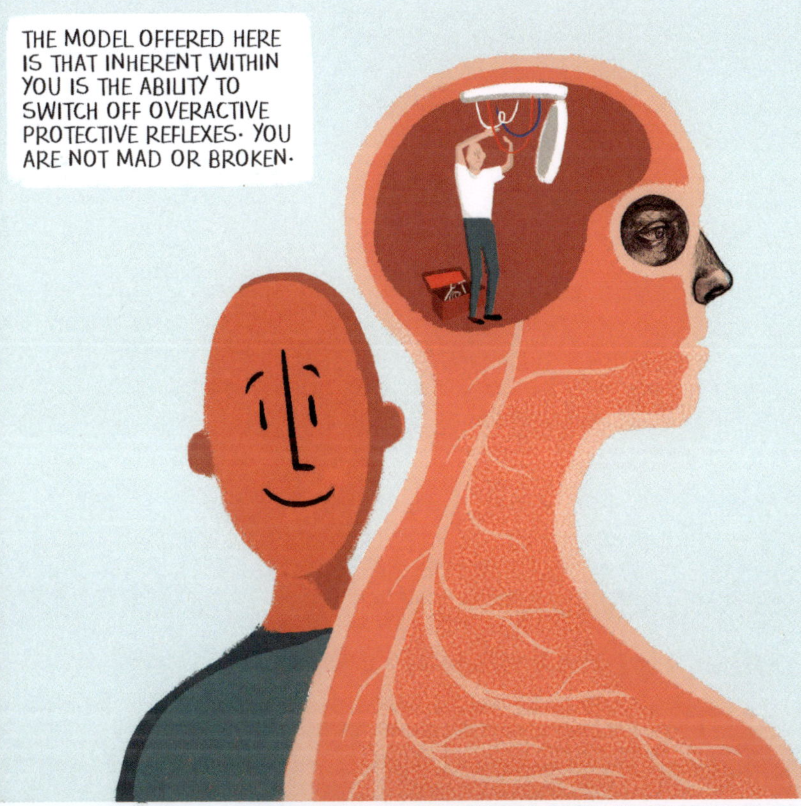

THE MODEL OFFERED HERE IS THAT INHERENT WITHIN YOU IS THE ABILITY TO SWITCH OFF OVERACTIVE PROTECTIVE REFLEXES. YOU ARE NOT MAD OR BROKEN.
RECALIBRATING THE SMOKE DETECTOR OF THE AMYGDALA IS A GREAT START TO HEALING TRAUMA.

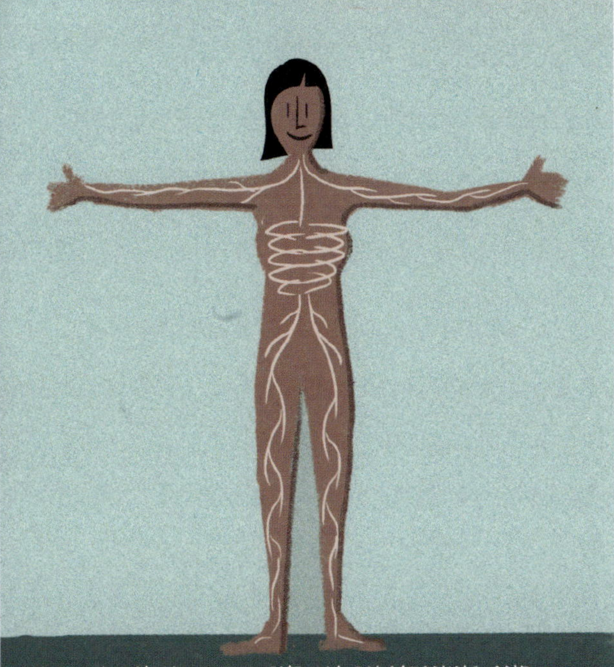

WHATEVER YOUR BELIEF SYSTEM ON MEANING AND PURPOSE IN LIFE, THERE IS THE VERY SIMPLE FACT OF THE BODY. YOU ARE IN A BODY RIGHT NOW. LEARN HOW IT WORKS AND EMBRACE THE MESSY, EARTHY GROUND OF FEELING.

LOSING CONTACT WITH YOUR BODY, AND YOUR ABILITY TO FEEL THE JOY AND GOODNESS INSIDE YOU, IS NOT A PRICE WORTH PAYING, WHATEVER HAS BEEN DONE TO YOU.

STRESS AND TRAUMA CHANGE HOW OUR BRAINS WORK. SQUEEZE ANY HUMAN HARD ENOUGH AND WE WILL BE OVERWHELMED. OFTEN WE DO NOT KNOW WHICH EXPERIENCES IMPRINTED OUR NERVOUS SYSTEM.

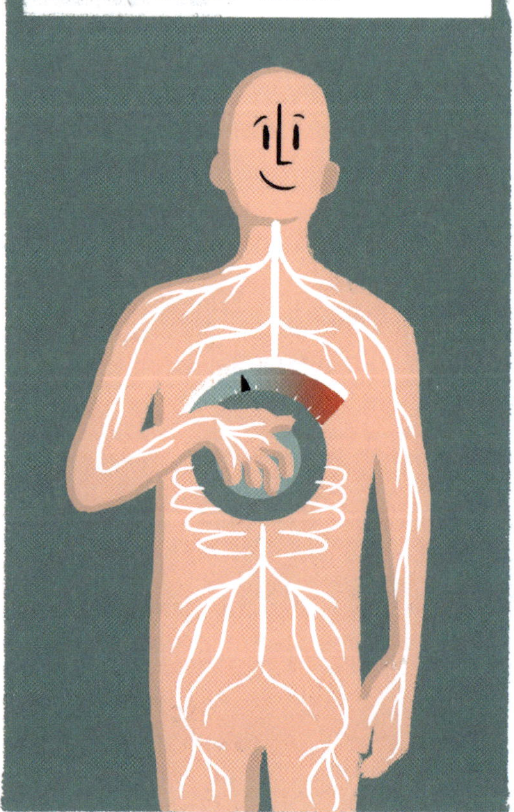

THE BEST WAY TO RESET THE OLD PARTS OF OUR BRAIN IS TO SLOWLY WAKE UP THE BODY. HEALING TRAUMA IS NOT ABOUT REMEMBERING, IT IS ABOUT SELF-REGULATING TO TURN DOWN INTENSE REACTIONS IN THE BODY.

BEING IN A BODY, WITHOUT CHRONIC TENSION PATTERNS AND A SENSITIZED BRAIN, WILL LEAD US TO BEING HAPPIER AND HEALTHIER.